P9-AQF-169

NJCMYQ

American Holidays / Celebraciones en los Estados Unidos

THANKSGIVING
DÍA DE ACCIÓN DE GRACIAS

Connor Dayton

Traducción al español: Eduardo Alamán

PowerKiDS
press™

New York

Published in 2012 by The Rosen Publishing Group, Inc.
29 East 21st Street, New York, NY 10010

First Edition

Editor: Jennifer Way   Traducción al español: Eduardo Alamán
Book Design: Julio Gil

Photo Credits: Cover, pp. 11, 24 (top left) Jon Feingersh/Blend Images/Getty Images; p. 5 © www.iStockphoto.com/Sean Locke; p. 7 Luis Marden/National Geographic/Getty Images; p. 9 SuperStock/Getty Images; pp. 12–13, 15, 17, 21, 23, 24 (bottom left, bottom right) Shutterstock.com; pp. 19, 24 (top right) gary718/Shutterstock.com.

Library of Congress Cataloging-in-Publication Data

Dayton, Connor.
  [Thanksgiving. Spanish & English]
  Thanksgiving = Día de Acción de Gracias / by Connor Dayton, Eduardo Alamán. — 1st ed.
      p. cm. — (American holidays = Celebraciones en los Estados Unidos)
  Includes index.
  ISBN 978-1-4488-6707-3 (library binding)
  1. Thanksgiving Day—Juvenile literature. I. Alamán, Eduardo. II. Title.
  GT4975.D3918 2012
  394.2649—dc23
                                        2011024284

Web Sites: Due to the changing nature of Internet links, PowerKids Press has developed an online list of Web sites related to the subject of this book. This site is updated regularly. Please use this link to access the list: www.powerkidslinks.com/amh/thanks/

Manufactured in the United States of America

CPSIA Compliance Information: Batch #WW12PK: For Further Information contact Rosen Publishing, New York, New York at 1-800-237-9932

Contents

Contenido

Americans celebrate Thanksgiving on the fourth Thursday in November. This holiday honors a 1621 Pilgrim **feast**.

El Día de Acción de Gracias se celebra en Estados Unidos el cuarto jueves de noviembre. Este día se recuerda el **banquete** de los colonos en 1621.

4

The Pilgrims came North America on the *Mayflower*. They landed in to Plymouth, Massachusetts, in 1620.

Los colonos llegaron a Norteamérica a bordo del *Mayflower*. Llegaron a Plymouth, en Massachusetts, en 1620.

Native Americans helped the Pilgrims during their first year. In 1621, the Pilgrims held the first Thanksgiving feast.

Los indígenas americanos ayudaron a los colonos durante su primer año. En 1621, los colonos celebraron el primer banquete de Acción de Gracias.

Families and friends get together on Thanksgiving. They eat and have fun.

Durante el Día de Acción de Gracias las familias y los amigos se reúnen. Las familias y los amigos comen y se divierten.

Turkey and **pumpkin** pie are two foods eaten on Thanksgiving. Illinois grows the most pumpkins.

En este día se acostumbra comer **pavo** y tarta de **calabaza**. En Illinois se producen la mayoría de las calabazas.

13

Sometimes people call Thanksgiving Turkey Day. Most Thanksgiving turkeys come from Minnesota.

Muchas personas llaman a esta celebración el Día del Pavo. La mayoría de estos pavos vienen de Minnesota.

Kids often make paper turkeys to put on the Thanksgiving table.

Con frecuencia, los chicos hacen pavos de papel para decorar la mesa del Día de Acción de Gracias.

Many people go to the Macy's Thanksgiving Day **Parade**, in New York City. It is shown on TV, too.

Muchas personas van al **desfile** del Día de Acción de Gracias de la tienda Macy's en Nueva York. Mucha gente también lo ve por televisión.

Some families play sports or games after their Thanksgiving dinner.

Muchas familias juegan algún deporte después de la cena del Día de Acción de Gracias.

Many families end Thanksgiving by watching football games on TV.

Muchas familias terminan el Día de Acción de Gracias mirando partidos de fútbol americano en televisión.

Words to Know / Palabras que debes saber

feast/ (el) banquete

parade/ (el) desfile

pumpkin / (la) calabaza

turkey / (el) pavo

24